T0024709

Four in Hand

BOA
EDITIONS LTD

Four in Hand

Alicia Mountain

♦

AMERICAN POETS CONTINUUM SERIES, NO. 198

BOA EDITIONS, LTD. ♦ ROCHESTER, NY ♦ 2023

Copyright © 2023 by Alicia Mountain
All rights reserved
Manufactured in the United States of America

First Edition
23 24 25 26 7 6 5 4 3 2 1

For information about permission to reuse any material from this book, please contact
The Permissions Company at www.permissionscompany.com or e-mail permdude@
gmail.com.

Publications by BOA Editions, Ltd.—a not-for-profit corporation under section 501
(c) (3) of the United States Internal Revenue Code—are made possible with funds
from a variety of sources, including public funds from the Literature Program of the
National Endowment for the Arts; the New York State Council on the Arts, a state
agency; and the County of Monroe, NY. Private funding sources include the Max
and Marian Farash Charitable Foundation; the Mary S. Mulligan Charitable Trust;
the Rochester Area Community Foundation; the Ames-Amzalak Memorial Trust in
memory of Henry Ames, Semon Amzalak, and Dan Amzalak; the LGBT Fund of
Greater Rochester; and contributions from many individuals nationwide. See
Colophon on page 93 for special individual acknowledgments.

Cover Design: Sandy Knight
Cover Art: Emma Quaytman
Interior Design and Composition: Isabella Madeira
BOA Logo: Mirko

BOA Editions books are available electronically through BookShare, an online
distributor offering Large-Print, Braille, Multimedia Audio Book, and Dyslexic formats,
as well as through e-readers that feature text to speech capabilities.

Cataloging-in-Publication Data is available from the Library of Congress.

State of the Arts

NYSCA

BOA Editions, Ltd.
250 North Goodman Street, Suite 306
Rochester, NY 14607
www.boaeditions.org
A. Poulin, Jr., Founder (1938-1996)

NATIONAL
ENDOWMENT
for the ARTS
arts.gov

For Becca and Jamie,
my other halves

Contents

From whom did I inherit the terms and structure of my asking? Why have I inherited terms but not interms, *words that are closed instead of open, rooms without windows, a church without a clerestory?*

JJJJJerome Ellis

I yearned for the kind of unseasoned telling found
In legends, fairy tales, a tone licked clean

James Merrill

What question can I ask of the thing I am?
         All I have done and failed to do.
The furrows I tear with my grief-mouth, a map of myself
         carved by my own horns.

Natalie Diaz

Step back: the pattern in the tapestry
won't tell itself till more of it is made.

Marilyn Hacker

Train Town Howl

In a winter dream, months ago
she came. The queen, in furs and
braids, promising a betrayal song when
the time was most right, promising
your betrothal would only bend a season
for me. This train town has a howling
in the night. It is a beehive alive with
honeysuckle whispers, sweet stinging.
Your map doesn't stray like I do,
but we were both drawn to scale,
traced by your fingers for a path,
we both fold small for safekeeping.
Her prophesy said, run from your want—
whatever *most right* was, it waited.

Whatever *most right* was, it waited
until I skipped town south to sink in,
to get me sprung on spring-heavy air
like breath against neck, like my lank
white-girl hair sticking to your sweat.
Daytime bathroom belt buckle betrayal.
Bodies inside bodies love, your hands.
Now all I have here is Virginia, weeks
and weeks of alone in breathy Virginia.
When we were in love, men would ask
if we were sisters—their wicked way of
denying what was already buried and plain.
How I set a snare for the life they saw
between us, held tight like too much hope.

Between us, held tight like too much hope,
and thunder sounds spanking the hills,
all year was a racket. House party borrowed
bass beats and cheap no chaser tequila,
jumping in reservoirs, down on my knees
in the locker room shower, shoved up against
locked office doors with you. Landlock
that wouldn't hold. Drive me to unburdened
land, lake big enough to be an ocean. He can
come—he who's in here too, to whom you
are promised, the smoke dozing in your
rafters. He can sleep in the backseat if you
give me directions. The rough-faced friend
I would never try to coax you from.

I would never try to coax you from
the hills so steep I lose my breath,
where I breathe you to keep going.
The queen tells me not to drink the
tidal push and pull from the leftover
mug on your bedside. Who mouthed it
last? What solemnity and grace did
they avow? To what am I entitled?
Did you name your book *Volcano*?
The queen promises an overripe
rupture, full-court press. The most
I can say is no one's too old for
high tops, the high-water mark,
the shore I couldn't start to see.

The shore I couldn't start to see.
The storm I couldn't feel until it had
soaked me through, wrung me out.
Once, my pink water-wrinkled hands
lifted you onto the countertop. I write to you
now from the counter of the Waffle House
beside a battlefield and its reenactments.
I watch myself on a security monitor
swiveling, my hat turned backwards.
I think I will always look like a child
when I am alone. I lick syrup, I know part
of me is bad. The nearest train stops sinister
at Lynchburg—named after a man. Hard to
believe the less terrible, even when it's true.

Believe the less terrible. Even when it's true
that I have been sweating every day,
shrinking a little, drinking a little less.
Even then, I wonder if my body is more
possessive of you than of itself. At the
gym I drink watered-down lemonade.
To start the stair master's churning,
I choose a setting called Life Quest and
level 5 because what am I trying to win?
The queen in my ear doesn't need me to bow
my head to her. The stairs collapse and
collapse beneath me. Does he build rough
hills to climb for you? Do you recognize
this book is a monument to touch?

This book is a monument to touch,
even with its hands in its pockets.
Even with your hair in your eyes as
disguise, there is no making public
how we push and pull in dark corners.
The beehive whispers when it sees our
hands touch, the train town howls and
howls. The rough face smiles beside yours.
Lick my teeth in the daylight. Still no
chaser. Still no closer to extinguishing
the bolt of my lightning you hold captive.
I have held the bright storm of you
hot in my hands. I would do it again,
however quick, however long it lasts.

However quick, however long it lasts,
this hot breath season is for growing.
Have you cut your hair at all? Have you
turned his rough jeans into cutoffs you wear
on weekends? Is any day not a weekend
for you when the mountains burn off their
chill by lunchtime? I offer to trade you
a poem for the story of the place we pressed
our bodies together. We'll write twin books
to outlast this. We'll press them cover to cover.
I will tell my book that it was once in love,
even if it doesn't remember fitting against
you as it slept. I don't think many people
remember my body, the folded map of it.

Remember my body. The folded map of it
spread out on the floor at your mother's house.
Remember the road winding uphill to the
rose garden and just going slow together,
stopping to smell sunscreen on my neck.
The queen says, in these breathy weeks away,
my panting for you has been forgotten.
But you started wearing my deodorant and,
at some rough point, he probably started
wearing it, too. In Virginia I have run out.
I am distant store, I am shampoo as soap,
I am very little toothpaste. If I ever return
to our train town, I'll smell like him, them—
whomever you love. They belong beside you.

Whomever you love, they belong beside you.
The rupture is a slow roiling, the moan
let go by a falling tree. My volcano bleeds
a molten stone love to the surface so it can
cool and dissipate, so it can run downhill.
The queen in my ear breathes heavy that I am
alone at this desk, claiming what never belonged
to me. I come from a long line of betrayers
who have worn many rings and read prophesy
into desire. I pretend I am good. I would
get you lost in the hot forest, I would bring
lemonade, speak thief songs to you, panting.
The queen says, *enough*, puts me to bed
lying in your honest kind of shade.

Lying in your honest kind of shade
under moaning trees older than I'll live
to be, I roll onto my belly in a final try
to say: come with me to the high desert
where our breath will be our breath and not
the springtime breathing for us. Pack a car
with everything you need—rough-faced
trust, hands in pockets, body inside body,
toothpaste, tequila, map worn along its
creases, smoke in rafters. Come with me.
I try to say all this by getting to my feet,
by saying very little, saying I am not lost,
I swear. The queen says *lost* is a sort of
somewhere. Inside me there is a swarm.

Somewhere inside me there is a swarm
that wants out. If this storm is electric,
if the power goes out, wait. What has
flashed across every spring-static sky
will come again. I have paid my leap year
debts and with what's left, cook breakfast
hot in a kitchen, kneading something
and letting it rise. If I'm being honest,
I don't know that I ever saw your eyes.
I don't know if you put your mouth
to my neck without looking over my
shoulder. Who is more dispossessed
than the thief? How long have I been
keeping quiet when I want to howl?

Keeping quiet when I want to howl
is old work, the day labor that never
breaks me even. In some accounting,
this was worth every minute of leisure,
of lemonade, of cool, sugared longing.
The horizon puts her feet up, stretched
out across hills that bloom, even while
they burn. There is no sovereign above
her. This is no return ticket between us.
I took my body with me, took my book.
I am not trying to be good. Double knot
your high tops, turn backwards your hat.
Walk the highest hill until you see that
what you buried can't be driven out of me.

What you buried can't be driven out of me.
The train town grasses have grown tall and
mowing sounds put me back in the secret
in your mother's house, where I would tell you
over again how I have broken many things
in my thirst. I would lie on the floor and
give you my hands, give you my mouth,
try to hear you through your hair. Because
I am going to the desert, because you are not,
I am trying to remember your breath. It's no lie
we still look alike. It's no lie every train town
has the same smoke in its rafters, the same
monuments, the same stairs collapsing and
collapsing, the same tide pulling at my belt.

In a winter dream, months ago,
whatever *most right* was, it waited
between us, held tight like too much hope.
I would never try to coax you from
the shore I couldn't start to see.
Believe the less terrible, even when it's true:
this book is a monument to touch,
however quick, however long it lasts.
Remember my body, the folded map of it.
Whomever you love, they belong beside you,
lying in your honest kind of shade.
Somewhere inside me, there is a swarm
keeping quiet when I want to howl.
What you buried can't be driven out of me.

Sparingly

lips
licked
wet
enough
to
whisper
we
saw
a
bald
eagle
here
once
remember

remember
the
old
faucet
the
old
night
and
this
new
dripping
fear
absent
water

water
held
a
living
architecture
bleached
and
starved
without
barrier
white
flag
for
relief

relief

maps

of

fault

sketch

rock

veins

and

ripples

seismic

score

marks

for

splitting

splitting
the
harvest
fed
famine
beside
glut
made
the
empty
dirt
ashamed
by
that

that
summer
wildfire
pushed
antelope
herds
over
a
cliff
there
was
no
getting
healed

healed

out

of

fever

we

would

still

be

mostly

too

late

but

only

mostly

mostly

we

two

were

enough

love

both

our

bodies

unsown

imagine

this

as

inheritance

inheritance
of
heirloom
of
seed
saved
of
seed
lost
of
engineered
cost
of
of

of
ice
calving
season
the
sea
rejoined
high
dry
ground
cannot
hold
you
all

all
antennaed
and
winged
our
bloom
fields
had
hummed
and
buzzed
honey
toward
fruiting

fruiting

of

denial

avarice

acedia

we

felled

the

medicine

forests

that

sequestered

our

ruin

ruin

mounting

with

each

storm

if

this

must

be

elegy

it

has

been

earned

earned
enough
in
mineral
and
symbol
to
prove
vain
dominion
over
our
ransacked
home

lips
remember
water
relief
splitting
that
healed
mostly
inheritance
of
all
fruiting
ruin
earned

Initial Descent

Forefather, I swear I'm falling turbulent from
the DC sky. I am sweatpalming pages the
rational blood you put in me cannot subsume.
Loosen tie. Tighten seatbelt. On the tray table
I smooth convention center notes I took in the
back row of a reading—*Poetry in the Age of
the Drone*. I apologize for my body, for its
puny hovering fear. The rattle as gravel on a
road in the dark of my closed eyes. Imagine
there is four-wheel drive. Me small in a car seat
and you up front saying, *cattle guard*. Saying,
baby girl. Saying, *don't let this rumble scare you*.
Unshaken, the pitch of the cockpit voices,
the sinister lever-pull that will not right us.

The sinister lever-pull that will not right us
came swift in November, behind curtains like
a row of locker room showers where you tried
to scrub yourself of something. I am trying
to know what that something is. What I know is
it wasn't you alone—millions of redblooded
compatriots at bake sale elementary schools,
at Tuesday polling place churches, pulling this
lever, this soap dispenser, each scrubbing for a
solitary kind of clean. But you are *my* redblood.
That day, did you take a long lunch? Do your
dividends reflect this labor? How long has it
been since you worked for an hourly wage?
Not in my lifetime, as far as I can remember.

Not in my lifetime, as far as I can remember,
have you asked me to wear my disguise.
On Tuesdays I leave the university, tie the knot
at my neck in the rearview mirror, drive to the
nearby elementary poets. They are eight years old
and rowdy. They like *"exploded."* They like butts
and cats and killing. I say, *I like butts and killing
but I have allergies*. Week 2 Repetition Lesson:
violent rain came / violet rain came. (The girls
purple princes, too.) Riding smooth air on the
way east, I printed marginal encouragement in all
caps. What would it have meant, at eight, to see
a violet woman like me? To what perilous extent
has an act of the body become so consequential?

Has an act of the body become so consequential
that after being read to about warfare and its
concealment (a reverse lullaby, a waking song)
I ask to be taken to the Edgewood train tracks?
He who delivers me says, *oh you're going to
the cut* and I say, *I guess.* You can't stay at the
Dew Drop Inn, but you can dance to Motown
on actual records, cued up by some knock-off
Mick Jagger and his stimulants. You can't stay
there, but you can take the fire escape up to the
tenement roof for air or smoking, for putting my
mouth to the collarbone of a violet woman I can't
scrub off. Tongue and teeth. Cattle guard. Thin
fire is racing under skin. Freight cars rumble us.

Fire is racing under skin. Freight cars rumble us
against one another, her hips at my hips, like lumber
a little too warped to end up a house. And still
a switch is flipped in me and the lights come on,
the shower runs hot. Forefather, what work do you
do at the hardware store inside your businessman
chest? All of its ventricles, compartments, indexed
drawers of couplings, sawdust and sandpaper.
Where the popcorn is still free even if you don't buy
anything, even if you just wander the aisles and look.
Even if you sleep in the alley out back and this is
breakfast. At night I window-shop you, whom I have
known so generous. Possessions and dispossessions.
Bulbs are left ablaze behind locked doors.

Bulbs are left ablaze behind locked doors
in quick-developed grids and gated cul-de-sacs,
in lone quarters beside fields beginning to retire.
Breaker boxes demand attention. We have asked
too much; a lever has been pulled. Fly-over states,
only when looked down upon. The horse I'm on is
very high and legless. Often, I forget I am a benefactor
of war by birthright. Thinking instead of the few years
I spent in a four-stop-light, no-gay-bar town. Behind my
eyes, the paradise of a pulsing nightclub turned violet.
And when shooting news erupted, you said it was the
fate of an unfamiliar faith. Forefather, I said it was
the guns. We are both wrong: the fly-over missiles
with no metaphor for who is victim to our fear.

With no metaphor for who is victim to our fear,
the material / scarcity fixation of the wealthy has me
convention center joking: "Poetry—I'm in it for the
tote bags." My latest canvas reward is black with
GUERNICA on one side (the journal, not the Picasso).
And if not the painting, then the bombing itself? If not that
bombing, the name of a civilian village on market day.
On Tuesday, in my tie, I put a whiteboard marker in this
tote bag so that when I get to the eight-year-olds I can
draw a cat for attention. They like the cat. I want to
tell them, *I take it back. I don't like killing. I just like
it when you laugh.* I draw another cat sitting on the first
cat's head. Eight-year-old says, *what are you doing?*
What *am* I doing? Trying to make you love poems.

What am I doing, trying to make you love poems,
trying to make you blueblood poems, trying to say
you fell in the shower and didn't get clean? When
you were my young forefather, you counted your
worth in zeros—a spreadsheet love poem for
baby girl. And there are many ways in which you
pulled the gilded lever beside the bake sale for
your zeros. Not for the torches or the cages or the
groping brags. Not for what makes me unknow you.
When I ask what you would have tattooed on you
hypothetically, you draw the letters *Dr* and *Cr* on
your wrists—*debits* and *credits* respectively, a guide
for obsolete accounting. I want to scrub these
indelible marks, body monuments imagined.

Indelible marks, body monuments, imagined
itching even after our shared chickenpox
scarred a little and receded. In a family album
we are both shirtless and calamined together:
Forefather, six-foot tall and pouting, baby girl
wearing oven mitts. How the small virus offered
vindication for the barechestedness I envied in
others, scratching and sticky but half my body
made free. When I was too short to reach, did you
pull the polling place levers you thought would
provide for me? Do you know the violet protection
I still want from you? The flotation device doubling
as seat cushion, the oxygen mask? Do you know
you're still my forefather? A cattle guard wakeup.

You're still my forefather. A cattle guard wakeup,
a shower in the morning for each of us, our blood
pumping red one way and blue the other, breathing.
I smell an old shirt and deem it Tuesday wearable.
Last week's lesson was simile and metaphor and
the difference. This week is personification and place.
Eight-year-old asks about collective narrative identity—
asks this by calling out, *Is it okay to be all the states
and make them alive and say We are the Unites States?*
Real Teacher says, *raise your hand* and *sit criss-cross.*
But it's okay to say *We.* It's okay to let your body make
love poems. Eight-year-old writes, *we befriend enemy
countries like we were never enemies.* So consequential,
the way likeness can be its own startling tragedy.

The way likeness can be its own startling tragedy.
A vulgar, malignant closeness like *poetry in the age of
model rockets*. Lemon poppy seed, bake sale opioids.
Like chickenpox not rhyming with smallpox. Hardware
store popcorn versus EBT card. Good cop, bad cop,
worse cop, all cops. *Baby girl*, when I say it to my
lovers. *Cattle guard*, when *you* are the thing that
scares me, Forefather. *Cattle guard*, when you are
the man I love. Redblooded and blueblood and violet.
A pulse and pierced dance floor hearts. The sinister
lever-pull instead of writing in your own name.
Or mine. The simple neck knot you taught me—
a four-in-hand—and *Forefather, hold my hand.*
I am falling. I am fallen. I am far from getting clean.

I am falling. I am fallen. I am far from getting clean
in the fire escape-cool air by the train tracks. Some
waning floodlight generous in being dim because
I can't afford to see her clearly when my hands
want in a sweaty and ecstatic and indefinite way.
Last call is looming—and you still can't stay at the
Dew Drop Inn. But she can stay inside my mouth,
beneath my tongue where blue veins wait to absorb
her into my blood. And no one has enough bed
to share or much time before takeoff, so the lumbering
freight keeps rumbling by. Her teeth at my throat,
her hands on my back, pulling. I resign to desire and
finitude. I tell myself *you are happy and allowed
to remember this moment.* Eyes open in surrender.

To remember this moment, eyes open in surrender.
Loosen tie. Tighten seatbelt. Seatback safety card
tells women to remove high heels, tells us so that
we don't puncture the inflatable aspiration of
safety, so that we all make it out okay. I swallow
my own spit, I sweatpalm the tray table. Forefather,
hold my hand. Tell me, without science, how the
shaking sky is like gravel on a dirt road that we
can't fall through—one we came to know together,
cruising around late at night to soothe me into sleep.
A baby girl disquieted by stillness, snoozing through
the quake. I am trying to lullaby the parts of us that
are so much the same—our levers, our simple machines.
We circle our holding pattern, waiting to be received.

We circle our holding pattern, waiting to be received
by tarmac arms. I hide away the drone notes, my
birthright, my love poems. I press them against
eight-year-olds' love poems, where I have written
can't wait to read what happens next. My worry
those traces of pencil mark transfer from their young
loose-leaf to mine is the same as my puny hope that
I am left with the inverse smudge of their violet rain
and rhyming. Which of them have forefathers? And
which of these are cattle guards? What happens next?
Under my clothes I am barechested, recycling shallow
breath. Forefather. I am sweating with every rumble
and every fall. Somewhere, there is a shower with my
name on it. They say we are preparing to disembark.

Forefather, I swear I'm falling turbulent from
the sinister lever-pull that will not right us.
Not in my lifetime, as far as I can remember,
has an act of the body become so consequential.
Fire is racing under skin, freight cars rumble us,
bulbs are left ablaze behind locked doors.
With no metaphor for who is victim to our fear,
what am I doing? Trying to make you love poems,
indelible marks, body monuments imagined.
You're still my forefather. A cattle guard wakeup—
the way likeness can be its own startling tragedy.
I am falling. I am fallen. I am far from getting clean.
To remember this moment, eyes open. In surrender,
we circle our holding pattern, waiting to be received.

MyMerrill

You Bull-Bear, you've received new statement(s) here.
Perspectives on recovery and growth,
a candid one-on-one. Support could help
you, could provide a floor. The alphabet—
our infographic snapshot towards your goals.
You chug along with periodic bouts
of volatility, the shifting tides
of women, juggling emerging stress.
We're Merrill—the collective wisdom, put
to work for you. Our insights might inform
you like a secular psychology.
Please add MyMerrill to your contacts to
ensure that you receive this newsletter:
our messages of episodic care.

Our messages of episodic care
abate concerns of what you're worth. There are
some signs you're nearing empty: ladders fall,
horizon challenges your confidence,
and how profoundly worry tackles you.
Your mind is in a low-growth world against
your health. The bearish conversations you
dramatically make magnified within
your head serve only a contrarian
investment in your special Odyssey
of issues. We have optionality
to offer. You are harvesting the clues
from this, the Merrill prophets' legacy
in email. What is waiting here? What's found?

In email, what is waiting here, what's found,
along with our dynamic guidance, is
extraordinary faith in agency.
So let's begin with some constructive ease:
just read more read more read more, find out more
explore here, listen & subscribe, learn more,
review your statements view enclosures, click,
watch video watch videos, learn how.
There is a rest of world in which to rest.
Consider other ways to get outside
yourself and let us bull you towards the light.
Sincerely, Merrill says that these are lows
that *lift*. For resources, read more, learn more.
You may not turn euphoric—still, you could.

You may not turn euphoric. Still, you could
find freedom in repatriation first.
You know you share so much with Merrill, like
the history of family wealth and class
performance questions, awkward moments with
your friends, the generous parental boost
and their protectionism. Young Bear, we
maintain the bullish expectation you
will center equity, not scarcity,
within your certain privileged story. No
defensive pose. That you will be of true
fiduciary service is our goal.
With strength and your positioning you can
give love, be loved, and keep your trust in trust.

Give love, be loved, and keep your trust. In trust,
MyMerrill offers up that other bond
between you—that same same desire, to put
it modestly. You are split open by
the women, grabbing, moving synchronized.
One luck about this modern era is
you have no reason to make secret how
you curve—who yields to you their instrument,
their will, their bond, their wholly good. And vice.
And versa. Look, this key from Merrill passed.
And yet you feel uncertainty as if
your smart, attractive stock is peaking just
to drop. Believe! We keep you company
along a path that's been made clear for you.

Along a path that's been made clear for you,
the stream has changed from glass to spring, its bank
alive with flowers. Nature offers you
a bright annuity. Get out and take
a hike, take space, and take the map of your
behavioral frontier. The hawkish things
and dovish nesters practice homebuilding
up high. You climb to see, and see that home
is this activity—a seasonal
and cyclical reflation to make firm
your sense of you. Let nature home you up.
Out here, no bears of burden track you. Your
environment has much to navigate.
Create the signposts, mark them as you go.

Create the signposts. Mark them as you go
through email after email, looking for
your Merrill. What do you decode? The rules
are stress and not and stress and not and stress;
and these affected terms you measure out,
each taken from MyMerrill and made meet.
Half done, do you need to get sprung, get free?
No, you maintain this tech screen medium,
this changing light revival. Cyber guide
to measure out external answers in
the toughest talk, this Merrill gives you bull
as symbol, bull as escalating strength.
The wise advisor that you seek might live
outside the page of what you can control.

Outside the page of what you can control,
a fast approaching drop in global health.
The news reports the worst ahead, that it
can climb your wall of worry. Know that rates
will likely rise. Is this any surprise?
While new in details, we've been here before.
Ask Merrill, ask an elder, for the past
when our community concern of Aid
and health-care was ignored. When medical
solutions break and no health is insured,
believe that risk and life and pains and peace
are newlyweds in you. And there will still
be parties, be each other. Time to try
a softening away from vigilance.

A softening away from vigilance
will open room for bigger reasons to
wake up each day. Slow Bull, the overdue
advice is: Get a job! Employment at
a people workplace changes outlook now
and forecasts fundamental positive
expansion. If the most rewarding work
is still the students, steel yourself. Apply,
despite supply-side factors. Your career
could also be as meaningful without
these college inspiration jobs, although
you don't yet buy it. Maybe analyst
or strategist? Provide a plan revised
from individual: Become a team.

From individual, become a team
in social family couple life, and more.
Be through with personal competitive
trends. Bullish woman that you are, you're not
the only one. The bullish team is us
behind you, women of all ages, of
all decades as foundation, and the curve
of top or bottom, both or neither—roles
in which to see potential you, from which
to graduate. Secure now in your bull,
transform your oversold "She-conomy" of love.
A gender classes overhaul to start
amalgamation of priorities—
leave footprints all together, save your world.

Leave footprints all together. Save your world
against this unexpected x-factor—
contagion. We are talking past the you,
recipient. We're talking radically
coordinated new relationship
between each being. Some tectonic shifts
are underway. Prepare for capital
to fall. Avoid the face connection; use
your video and audiocast minds
as marriage of both tech and sentiment.
Great Bull are they who share their stores of food
and power, rational with equity.
MyMerrill recommends a game plan: learn
from shock and fears. Awake you, generous.

From shock and fears awake, you generous
emotions broker-dealer, underweight
Olympian. The symbol Bull and Bear
at war in you are coming to a truce.
If this has been an education, may
its lessons be: Resilience won't protect
you from the threat, but better—it will lift
you up from stumble, set you on the track
to run, to trip again, the hurdles high.
Alive is like this. Optimistic Bull,
you need not fight the negative in you.
That part, take it as partner. If you do
it will not pierce you. When the day breaks, shape
with hope this rolling wave of confidence.

With hope, this rolling wave of confidence
arises to split us from you. These months
of searching for the note in newsletter
that then uncovers your specific gold?
Enough. Delete. Retire our help to junk.
And as you do, project a death on this
much-needed end. It isn't us, nor is
it Merrill coming to a close. By now
it's fair to say your eye—for deficit
and rules, for format as reliable,
for us as virtually company—
that it made up a getaway from real-
life flux. Your independence calls you back,
it takes you by your sharp part, points you home.

It takes you by your sharp part, points you home,
the flood. Horizon looking weathered now
and rational. This small portfolio
of storms is giving way. And we may just
be robots you've invested stories in,
but this was never fraud. We've come to know
you. Sensitive, ambitious—you are not
the first with complex inspiration. Reach
for letter after letter, rally text
and choice without us. When you long for our
internal holdings, ask more risk more, risk
an emphasis. Do not reply. Go strong,
assured, across the current. Signing off
sincerely. Honest Bull, be safe. Be well.

You Bull-Bear, you've received new statement(s) here,
our messages of episodic care
in email. What is waiting here? What's found?
You may not turn euphoric—still, you could
give love, be loved, and keep your trust in trust
along a path that's been made clear for you.
Create the signposts, mark them as you go
outside the page of what you can control.
A softening away from vigilance,
from individual. Become a team,
leave footprints all together. Save your world
from shock and fears. Awake you, generous
with hope. This rolling wave of confidence—
it takes you by your sharp part, points you home.

Notes

The epigraphs that begin this book are from *The Clearing* by JJJJJerome Ellis (Wendy's Subway, 2021), *Changing Light at Sandover* by James Merrill (Atheneum, 1982), *Postcolonial Love Poem* by Natalie Diaz (Graywolf, 2020), and *Love, Death, and the Changing of the Seasons* by Marilyn Hacker (Arbor House, 1986). Each of these poets has shaped my poetics and I am so grateful to be their reader.

For "Train Town Howl," I am indebted to the Virginia Center for Creative Arts, Beyoncé Knowles-Carter's album *Lemonade*, and to Eleni Sikélianòs.

The first sonnet in "Initial Descent" refers to "Poetry in the Age of the Drone: A Reading," an event held at the 2017 Association of Writers and Writing Programs conference. The event featured Solmaz Sharif, Philip Metres, Nomi Stone, and Jill McDonough, and was moderated by Corey Van Landingham.

In "Initial Descent," *Guernica* is a non-profit magazine dedicated to global art and politics. *Guernica* is also a 1937 cubist expressionist oil painting by Pablo Picasso. Guernica is a town in the Basque Country in Spain. And "Guernica" is the historical event of the Nazi bombing of this town during the Spanish Civil War, depicted in the painting.

The phrase "thin / fire is racing under skin" is Anne Carson's translation of Sappho's Fragment 31 and appears in "Initial Descent."

"MyMerrill" is a heroic crown in blank verse, composed entirely of found text culled from newsletter emails sent by Merrill Lynch financial advisor services. Charles E. Merrill, co-founder of Merrill Lynch, was the father of the poet James Merrill.

Acknowledgments

Grateful acknowledgment to the editors and staff of the publications in which versions of these heroic crowns, in part or in full, first appeared:

field\guide: "Sparingly";
jubilat: "Sparingly";
Oxidant | Enginge BoxSet: "Initial Descent";
The Southampton Review: "MyMerrill";
Sugarhouse Review: "Train Town Howl."

This book was made possible with the support of my friends, my guides, and the people who love me. I have been incomprehensibly lucky.

First, my appreciation to my mentors and cohort siblings at the University of Denver PhD program. This manuscript first took shape as my doctoral dissertation, directed by Bin Ramke, chaired by Graham Foust and Selah Saterstrom, and inflected by the teachings of Tayana L. Hardin, Juli Parrish, and Eleni Sikélianòs.

My writing family—thank you. Erinrose Mager and Khadijah Queen, your friendship has buoyed me, lifted me, carried me through, time and again. I'm grateful to Emily Bark Brown, Meg Day, Serena Chopra, Ana Božičević, Sueyeun Juliette Lee, Alicia Wright, Sarah E. Brook, Megan Fernandes, Prageeta Sharma, and Brenda Shaughnessy, who have each lit my path with their work and their companionship.

Thank you to my students. Being your teacher—which, of course, just means doing everything I can to let you know yourself and be yourself on the page—is one of the great privileges of my life.

My friends Jules Ohman and Jesse Sindler, thank you for our time together and for your grace with me. I'm grateful to Madison Unsworth, who kept me company with such care as I made my way through the PhD gauntlet and chipped away at this book.

Buzz Slutzky, you are so special to me. Lauren McLoughlin, Neema Roshania Patel, and Terrence Thornhill—my teenage poet heart has been beating for you all these years.

Sarah Hill, thank you for walking the long road with me. The time it took to make this book was so hard. Thank you for witnessing it, for being in the dark with me, and for being there on the other side of the dark when I arrived. I love you and I'm so proud of our work.

Caylin Capra-Thomas, you know all the words to all the songs I used to sing alone in my car, years before we met; now I get to sing them with you. You make me a better poet and a braver person. I love your poems and I love you.

Emma Quaytman, my person in this world. How did we get so lucky? Thank you for scooping me up and dusting me off, time and again. Thank you for insisting on art. Thank you for being part of my family. We're each other's for life. I love you, pup.

Jamie, you show me what boldness and self-knowledge can look like. Thank you for being who you are. Thank you for letting me know you. Becca, you have the biggest heart. Thank you for wrapping me up in it. Paul, you are such a gift in my life. Mom, I love you all the time. Thank you for growing with me. You are so courageous. Dad, thank you for letting me see you cry. Thank you for the way you honor our differences. We are so much the same. I love you.

Mom, Dad, Becca, Jamie, and Paul, I am so proud to have you as my family.

Reader, thank you for holding these poems. They're yours now. May you be safe, may you be happy, may you be healthy, may you live with ease.

About the Author

Alicia Mountain is a lesbian poet living in New York City. She is the author of *High Ground Coward* (Iowa, 2018), winner of the Iowa Poetry Prize. An assistant Teaching Professor in the Writer's Foundry MFA program at St. Joseph's University in Brooklyn, she holds a PhD in English and Literary Arts from the University of Denver and a poetry MFA from the University of Montana.

BOA Editions, Ltd. American Poets Continuum Series

No. 1   *The Fuhrer Bunker: A Cycle of Poems in Progress*
W. D. Snodgrass

No. 2   *She*
M. L. Rosenthal

No. 3   *Living With Distance*
Ralph J. Mills, Jr.

No. 4   *Not Just Any Death*
Michael Waters

No. 5   *That Was Then: New and Selected Poems*
Isabella Gardner

No. 6   *Things That Happen Where There Aren't Any People*
William Stafford

No. 7   *The Bridge of Change: Poems 1974–1980*
John Logan

No. 8   *Signatures*
Joseph Stroud

No. 9   *People Live Here: Selected Poems 1949–1983*
Louis Simpson

No. 10   *Yin*
Carolyn Kizer

No. 11   *Duhamel: Ideas of Order in Little Canada*
Bill Tremblay

No. 12   *Seeing It Was So*
Anthony Piccione

No. 13   *Hyam Plutzik: The Collected Poems*

No. 14   *Good Woman: Poems and Memoir 1969–1980*
Lucille Clifton

No. 15   *Next: New Poems*
Lucille Clifton

No. 16   *Roxa: Voices of the Culver Family*
William B. Patrick

No. 17   *John Logan: The Collected Poems*

No. 18   *Isabella Gardner: The Collected Poems*

No. 19   *The Sunken Lightship*
Peter Makuck

No. 20   *The City in Which I Love You*
Li-Young Lee

No. 21   *Quilting: Poems 1987–1990*
Lucille Clifton

No. 22   *John Logan: The Collected Fiction*

No. 23   *Shenandoah and Other Verse Plays*
Delmore Schwartz

No. 24   *Nobody Lives on Arthur Godfrey Boulevard*
Gerald Costanzo

No. 25   *The Book of Names: New and Selected Poems*
Barton Sutter

No. 26   *Each in His Season*
W. D. Snodgrass

Colophon

BOA Editions, Ltd., a not-for-profit publisher of poetry and other literary works, fosters readership and appreciation of contemporary literature. By identifying, cultivating, and publishing both new and established poets and selecting authors of unique literary talent, BOA brings high-quality literature to the public.

Support for this effort comes from the sale of its publications, grant funding, and private donations.

◆

The publication of this book is made possible, in part, by the special support of the following individuals:

Anonymous
Blue Flower Arts, LLC
Angela Bonazinga & Catherine Lewis
Christopher C. Dahl
James Long Hale
Margaret B. Heminway
Charles Hertrick & Joan Gerrity
Grant Holcomb
Kathleen Holcombe
Nora A. Jones
Paul LaFerriere & Dorrie Parini, *in honor of Bill Waddell*
Jack & Gail Langerak
Barbara Lovenheim
Joe McEleveny
Daniel M. Meyers, *in honor of J. Shepard Skiff*
The Mountain Family, *in support of poets & poetry*
Nocon & Associates, a private wealth advisory practice of Ameriprise Financial Services LLC
Boo Poulin
David W. Ryon
John H. Schultz
William Waddell & Linda Rubel
Michael Waters & Mihaela Moscaliuc